W9-BMV-252

MAKING CONTACT

Virginia Satir

Celestial Arts
Berkeley, California

Illustrations by Pedro J. Gonzalez
Design by Brenton Beck

Copyright © 1976 by Virginia Satir

Celestial Arts
P.O. Box 7327
Berkeley, California 94707

No part of this book may be reproduced by any
mechanical, photographic, or electronic process,
or in the form of a phonographic recording, nor
may it be stored in a retrieval system, transmit-
ted, or otherwise copied for private or public
use without the written permission of the
publisher.

Library of Congress Catalog Card No.: 75-28768
ISBN: 0-89087-119-1

First printing: August 1976
Made in the United States of America

19   20   21   -   90

I believe
The greatest gift
I can conceive of having
from anyone
is
to be seen by them,
heard by them,
to be understood
and
touched by them.
The greatest gift
I can give
is
to see, hear, understand
and to touch
another person.
When this is done
I feel
contact has been made.

God, give me the serenity to accept the things I cannot change
The courage to change the things I can and the wisdom to tell the difference.

Prelude

We "made contact" with Virginia Satir about 18 years ago, shortly before she and doctors Don Jackson and Jules Riskin formed the Mental Research Institute in Palo Alto, California. Since 1955 she had been working with the director of the Illinois State Psychiatric Institute, Dr. Kalman Gyarfas, in teaching psychiatric residents the new ideas of working with families instead of only the hospitalized person.

She came to the Mental Research Institute in 1959 to do research in the relationship of family interaction and its relationship to health and illness of its members. One year later, Virginia began a training program for family therapy. She continued to develop her innovative and, at that time, unorthodox techniques of helping people. These techniques are now in use all over the world.

Virginia was, and still is, a pioneer in family therapy—working with the whole family when one of its members has problems instead of concentrating on the troubled member. She has reached millions through her very successful books, *Peoplemaking* and *Conjoint Family Therapy*, and seminars and workshops. Her interest in all areas of "people-service" has led her to become consultant to various governmental agencies, including the Bureau of Indian Affairs, state and federal hospitals, state departments of welfare, the U.S. Army and Navy, the Veterans Administration, private clinics, medical schools, psychiatric departments in universities in the United States and in Israel, Venezuela, Sweden, Norway, Canada, and Germany. Recently she has been most interested in organizing an international traveling university which she envisions as "The University for the Development of Being More Human."

During the years of our friendship, we have been impressed with Virginia's unending quest for greater understanding of human potential and interaction, as well as her equally tireless efforts to reach and teach as many people as is humanly possible. There are always more people ready and eager for her seminars and workshops than there is room.

Today when everyone is scurrying about trying to find solutions to their problems, to improve themselves and their relationships with others, clear concise concepts are needed. Instead of new jargon, instead of statistical abstractions, instead of gurus and mass behavior modification, we need to concern ourselves with the essentials—the BARE BONES of interpersonal relationships.

Over the years Virginia's concepts and

techniques have been analyzed, adopted and adapted, interpreted and translated, to the point of sometimes obscuring her intended purposes. Now there is a need to restate the essence of her work, to present that essence directly to those of us who want to know and understand the universal principles of "peoplemaking."

Virginia has had an important effect on our lives and work, our publishing direction has been influenced by her teachings and actions. We are especially pleased to be able—after 18 years of observing, sharing, partaking in each other's development—to present in clear and concise terms, Virginia Satir's principles in a way in which each of us can put them to work for ourselves. We feel the BARE BONES series is the next best thing to having a chat with Virginia herself.

Hal and Ruth Kramer
Publishers

Acknowledgments

Very special thanks to George Young, Trae Boxer, Nancy MacDonald, Marlyn Keating and Ruth Nichols for helping to make this book what it is, and especially to Hal Kramer and his staff at Celestial Arts for their patience and creativity.

Introduction

I have been traveling about the world for forty years now. This time has given me the possibility of being in contact with thousands of people from different walks of life. Many of these people came because they wanted help with their problems in living, or because they wanted to learn how to better help the people who had these problems.

I have often heard, "Virginia, you have helped me to find so many good things for myself. Won't you write down how you make that happen?" I have now heard this so often that I no longer feel that I can continue to ignore the request.

I feel a deep humility for the expression of appreciation. I also feel tremendously awed by the immensity of the task. Memories flooded me of hours and hours, during days and nights, that I had spent with people, preparing them for the many little steps they had to make in order to take the risks that would result in the changes they wanted. I remembered the carefulness and patience with which I needed to proceed so that while they were facing the pain and uncertainty that often goes along with making changes, there would be no injury to their self-esteem along the way.

I know that books are not substitutes for people. However, I remembered the many times when a particular book read at a time when I was in a receiving mood, opened up new possibilities which resulted in my taking new directions for myself.

If I wrote this book simply and directly, it might have similar results for others.

This is what I have done. The framework of this book is the BARE BONES of the possible, which I believe applies to *all* human beings.

You, the reader, can flesh out the framework to fit you.

Virginia Satir

What I am presenting
Is all against a background
Of a Universal human experience.
We are all born little,
And of a specific man and woman.
Between birth and today,
Everyone has accumulated
Vast experience
Which we know as the past.
In a way,
All things you have done
Up to the present,
If you are still around,
Have worked.
The question again is,
What is the price
and
Could the price be lower . . .

MAKING CONTACT

Making contact is not a game of winning your point and living happily ever after. It is a means of dealing honestly and sharing humanly your human issues and concerns. It is a way of maintaining your integrity and nurturing your growing self-esteem and in the long run strengthening your relationship with yourself and others.

Developing this kind of wisdom is a lifetime search. It calls for much patience with ourselves. Knowing ourselves and making contact with others is the key in this search.

The more full and complete the contact that we make with ourselves and each other, the more possible it is to feel loved and valued, to be healthy and to learn how to be more effective in solving our problems.

My poem, *Goals for Me*, is my expression of how I am trying to accomplish this.

Goals For Me

I want to love you without clutching,
appreciate you without judging,
join you without invading,
invite you without demanding,
leave you without guilt,
criticize you
without blaming,
and help you without insulting.

If I can have the same from you
then we can truly meet and
enrich each other.

Making contact involves two people at a time
and three parts. Each person in contact with
himself or herself and each in contact with the
other.

Let's look at a familiar picture:

External Dialogue
So what's the matter with you? . . .
Internal Dialogue
My God, she looks so glum I must have done something wrong. But, if she really loved me she wouldn't look like that . . .

External Dialogue
Nothing . . .
Internal Dialogue
I feel like hell! He doesn't care. If he really loved me he would read my mind and not ask . . .

Where do you suppose they will be one hour from now?

This external dialogue is what passes for contact much of the time.

I have seen this same dialogue go on in all the cultures, income levels, and countries in my travels. This makes me suspect that this is a universally used pattern.

It isn't that it was in our genes when we were born, it only reflects our learning over time.

Since it was learned, then, at any point in our lives we can change. Being willing to learn something new will make the difference.

In the first picture, the words carry very little helpful information and seem more like an attack than a useful contact.

The inside experience of each person seems to be very different from their outside expression. Each in their insides seems to feel lonely, rejected and helpless without too much hope of changing that condition.

How could two people who care about each other make sense of what is going on?

The way in which they are positioned with their backs to each other, one standing and the other sitting, helps them to continue feeling what they are already feeling.

Besides, neither of them probably has a very accurate idea of how they are sounding to the other. They have to guess, and often this guess is in the negative.

These people are really only meeting masks of each other.

It is as though the persons believed that they were not worth being listened to, and felt too unworthy to find out. "Who cares about me" is what it often comes down to. That is a very heavy load to carry.

In the second picture, the same situation is handled quite differently.

First, the two people are positioned so that they are face-to-face at eye level and arm's length and have a much better chance of actually seeing and hearing each other.

And, they are saying what is going on inside themselves. Inside feelings and outside expressions of those feelings match.

Masks are not needed. The honesty shown reflects the loving between the pair; the "Who-cares-about-me" feeling is not present. The self-esteem of each is not injured. It might only be a little uncomfortable. Now they can use their energies for making useful contact and begin building together.

Anything that injures self-esteem reduces the opportunity to make good contact.

Preserving and enhancing self-esteem is my aim for myself and others around me. We can then come from a strong place to each other.

People who can injure another's self-esteem do so through carelessness and being unaware. Much of it is unintentional.

Contact has a better chance of being made facing each other at eye level and arm's length, and talking straight (congruent).

When you sit like that and look like that, I feel very bad and I would like to know what's the matter. Did I do something wrong?

I feel like hell! It's not anything **you** did. I wish you could read my mind and not ask me because I feel embarassed to feel like this. I just don't like myself.

Self-esteem is the center of all our being and it is essential to living a free life.

To make self-esteem more possible and contact more satisfying we need ways to enhance it.

My idea of how it can happen begins with the philosophy expressed in the following poem.

I Am Me

*In all the world, there is no one else
exactly like me.
There are persons who have some parts
like me,
but no one adds up exactly like me.
Therefore, everything that comes out of
me is authentically mine because I alone
chose it.
I own everything about me—my body,
including everything it does;
my mind, including all its thoughts and
ideas;
my eyes, including the images of all they
behold;
my feelings, whatever they may be—
anger, joy, frustration, love, disappoint-
ment, excitement;
my mouth, and all the words that come
out of it, polite, sweet or rough, correct
or incorrect;*

my voice, loud or soft;
and all my actions, whether they be to
others or to myself.

I own my fantasies, my dreams, my
hopes, my fears.
I own all my triumphs and successes, all
my failures and mistakes.
Because I own all of me, I can become
intimately acquainted with me.
By so doing I can love me and be
friendly with me in all my parts.

I can then make it possible for all of me
to work in my best interests.
I know there are aspects about myself
that puzzle me, and other aspects that I
do not know.
But as long as I am friendly and loving
to myself, I can courageously and
hopefully look for the solutions to the
puzzles and for ways to find out more
about me.
However I look and sound, whatever I
say and do, and whatever I think and
feel at a given moment in time is me.
This is authentic and represents where I
am at that moment in time.
When I review later how I looked and

sounded, what I said and did, and how I
thought and felt, some parts may turn
out to be unfitting.

I can discard that which is unfitting, and
keep that which proved fitting, and in-
vent something new for that which I
discarded.
I can see, hear, feel, think, say, and do.
I have the tools to survive, to be close
to others, to be productive, and to make
sense and order out of the world of
people and things outside of me.
I own me,
and therefore I can engineer me.
I am me
and I am okay.

What this poem is all about I call Self-esteem.

"This sounds so simple. Why is it so hard to
do?" people say.

Let us remember that what we are now doing, we have probably been doing for a long
time. It is very familiar and very likely has
become a habit.

Like all habits, it comes automatically and
we stop noticing.

"That's the way I am," I hear so often. "How
could I be otherwise?"

Anything that is familiar is hard to recognize, and hard to let go even when that way is painful or gives trouble.

Did you ever hear of the man who was released from prison after twenty years confinement? Who after a few weeks being outside, asked to return. The outside was too unfamiliar. Prison with its familiarity seemed preferable. This is, of course, an extreme example.

"After all, how do I know that something new will be any different?" The answer is "You don't know unless you try."

Even though many people long for something better, given the opportunity to have it, they often have to struggle against the "comfort" of familiarity. Once you leave the familiar, obviously you get into the unknown, which is a scary part for most of us.

This is where the pain of change is, giving up the familiar to plunge into the unknown. This pain is often called anxiety or insecurity.

A very important fact about enhancing self-esteem is that we don't have to grow another leg, change our color, get a million dollars, be a different age or sex, or get different parents.

We need only to change our attitudes and learn new personal skills. It can happen to everyone.

The parts we need we already have. It is a case of getting acquainted with them and understanding and expanding our use of them.

What makes it possible to enhance our feelings of self-esteem is our willingness to be open to new possibilities, to try them on for size, and then, if they fit us, to practice using them until they are ours.

To start the process I have developed something I have called . . .

The Five Freedoms

The freedom to see and hear what is here instead of what should be, was, or will be.

The freedom to say what one feels and thinks, instead of what one should.

The freedom to feel what one feels, instead of what one ought.

The freedom to ask for what one wants, instead of always waiting for permission.

The freedom to take risks in one's own behalf, instead of choosing to be only "secure" and not rocking the boat.

Congruence

Changing is, first, a matter of becoming honest with your feelings. Being emotionally honest, is the heart of making contact. I call this condition of being emotionally honest *congruence*.

The sad thing is that most people take emotional dishonesty for granted and are unaware that anything else is possible. They really think they are doing what they ought to do and then suffer unnecessarily as a result.

Congruence is possible for all human beings. You are your most important resource. You always carry yourself with you.

Congruence is also a matter of taking risks. A simple definition of taking a risk is doing something you have never done before or doing the same thing in a new way.

Have you ever heard the story about the young bride who was preparing roast beef. Her bridegroom exclaimed, with considerable surprise, when she carefully cut her roast in half and placed it in two pans, "Why do you do that?"

She answered very confidently, "That's the way to do it, my mother always did it that way."

The bridegroom, aware that he was no expert on cooking, yet suspicious of this logic, decided to do some research. He hastened to his mother-in-law and found that she indeed did roast beef the same way, stating, "That's the way to do it. My mother always did it that way." Fortunately for our story, her mother was still alive, so he hastened to her home and told her his story. She listened attentively and then with great amusement and surprise, she said, "Oh, my goodness! I always had so many people to feed and I had only small pans, so I had to cut the roast in smaller pieces to fit the pans."

How much do you still cut into two pieces and put into small pans, even though you have bigger pans around?

At first glance it might seem that making the kind of changes you want will be a monumental task. In one way it is—if you think about doing it all at once, or if you have to do it in a special way.

If you think of doing it a piece at a time and in the best way that fits you, then it is easier.

When I approach the matter of making change, I look in four directions:

1. How do I feel about myself? (Self-esteem)

2. How do I get my meaning across to others? (Communication)

3. How do I treat my feelings?

   Do I own them or put them on someone else?

   Do I act as though I have feelings that I do not or that I have feelings that I really don't have? (Rules)

4. How do I react to doing things that are new and different? (Taking risks)

One change already influences other parts. That means we can start anywhere . . .

Here is my picture of how these parts fit together. They are really all connected.

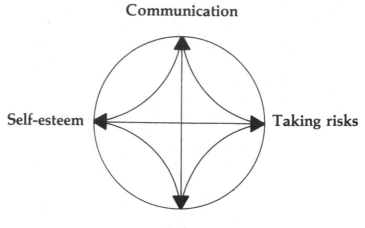

Communication

Self-esteem

Taking risks

Rules

Make a change in your Rules and you already influence your Self-esteem, your Communication and your Risk-taking.

Make a change in your Communication and you already influence your Risk-taking, your Rules and your Self-esteem.

Make a change in your Self-esteem and you already influence your Communication, your Risk-taking and your Rules.

Make a change in your Risk-taking and you

already influence your Rules, your Self-worth and your Communication.

You can start anywhere and something will change. Each change affects the other parts.

Sometimes it works a little like a mobile. Change one part and another one or two go out of balance. Sometimes people feel afraid when this happens. All that it means is that you have disturbed the old balance and you have new balancing to do.

Each part has infinite possibilities. Once we start the process of changing, if we keep nurturing it, we become more and more finely tuned as people who can make creative, loving and real contact with ourselves and others.

Human beings do not die easily, the will to live is strong. Every communication has the power of personal survival in it. I am using survival in the sense of what one does to *matter* and to *count*.

The question becomes: Is there a better way to survive without threatening our bodies, our relationships, and our souls. I think there is.

When people do not feel congruent their relationships become a series of power plays and win/lose operations, thus making little opportunity for them to have good relationships with each other.

When relationships consist mainly of power plays then power has to be misused.

How often have we heard . . .

"He has the courage of his convictions."

"He has the courage to say where he stands."

"He has the courage to take risks."

This power is scary but it isn't destructive . . .

People need to feel powerful because it insures the need to survive. Most of our communication follows that need.

To feel we can survive we need to feel powerful. That means we need to feel strong. Feeling strong is essential to having self-esteem. So to have self-esteem, we need to feel strong and that means to feel powerful. We need to feel that we count. To do that, we need to develop personal responsibility and create ways to help it happen with other people.

Many people are afraid of power because to them it means only force. I think of power as energy, something that can be used, channeled and directed toward destructive and constructive ends.

We can choose, and choose responsibly. Owning my power is the beginning of my becoming a choice-maker for me and becoming a responsible human being.

Living the *Five Freedoms* is, in my opinion, the strongest position of personal power that one can have.

Power/energy takes many forms . . .

It takes power/energy to keep our body upright and to move it. Most people understand that. It takes power-energy to protect ourselves. Most people accept that.

It also takes energy to connect with another person. Most people hope for this, but many people give it away by making the other person responsible for them.

We have at least two main ways to go. One is to make the other person responsible for our use of power and the other is to make ourselves responsible. Making real contact means that we make ourselves responsible for what comes out of us. This is an outcome of congruence. If we believe or act as though the other person is responsible for us, it puts our power in the other person's hands. "You make it possible for me to live," is the same use of power as "You are responsible for my dying."

One sounds positive, the other negative, but it still means the same thing: "I have given my power to you." In this case one person has to be up and the other down, and therefore no real contact can take place.

Let's look specifically at **communication**, one of the key parts in shaping what kind of contact is made.

A simple definition of communication is the giving and receiving of meaning between any two people. The questions become . . .

What meaning is made?

How is it given?

How is it received?

What happens to each person as a result and what happens to the relationship?

I made up an old saying . . .

> *Communication is to relationship what breathing is to maintaining life . . .*

Within this context, it is easier to understand why there is so much pain in human relationship.

Everyone breathes and everyone communicates. The question is how and what happens as a result?

There are four types of communicating that often go along with people who have low opinions of themselves, who have not yet learned to live their *Five Freedoms*.

These types of communications have a negative influence on the body, thus they affect physical health. They box in relationships so they become destructive, dead, distant and frustrating.

They limit the use of an individual's resources and ability to build with one another. They frustrate the dreams one has for oneself and increase the amount of fear and dependency. I have called them . . .

Placating

Blaming

Super Reasonable

Irrelevant

Placating

I'm always doing everything wrong!

Inside-Top Level:
I must keep everyone happy so they will love me!

Inside-Lower Level:
I'm really unlovable . . .

(My stomach hurts . . .)

Blaming

You never do anything right!

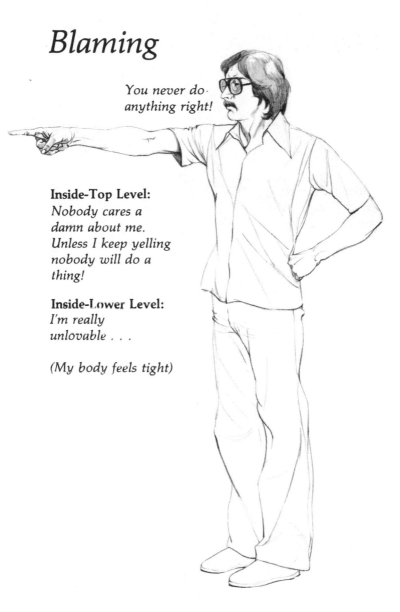

Inside-Top Level:
Nobody cares a damn about me. Unless I keep yelling nobody will do a thing!

Inside-Lower Level:
I'm really unlovable . . .

(My body feels tight)

Super Reasonable

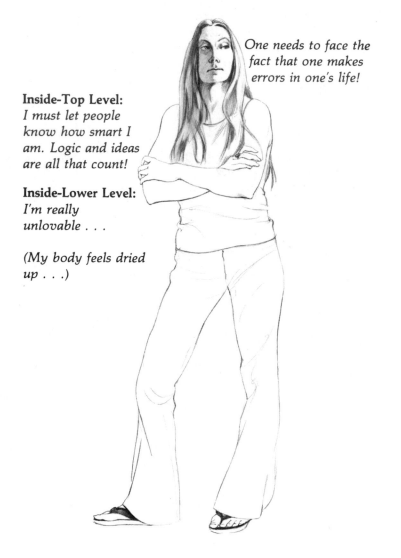

One needs to face the fact that one makes errors in one's life!

Inside-Top Level:
I must let people know how smart I am. Logic and ideas are all that count!

Inside-Lower Level:
I'm really unlovable . . .

(My body feels dried up . . .)

Irrelevant

Ho Ho, balance!
Errors, errors!!
Anybody got a
penny? . . .

Inside-Top Level:
*I will get attention
no matter to what
extremes I have
to go!*

Inside-Lower Level:
*I'm really
unlovable . . .*

*(My body feels out
of balance . . .)*

I look at these ways of communicating as being the ways we learned to survive physically and emotionally as we were growing up.

Because they represent our survival, they are also the means by which we manage our power and try to enhance our self-esteem.

We all need power and we all have it even though we might not recognize it. The questions are how do we show it, how do we use it, and what happens to us as a result?

Do we do it by placating? pleasing people enough so at least they will let us live?

Do we do it by blaming? forcing people to obey us so we will feel safe, at least for the moment?

Do we do it by being super reasonable? drowning people in words, boring them with endless explanations, and frustrating them by showing no feelings?

Do we do it by being irrelevant? keeping people so busy by introducing so many unconnected things that they feel dizzy and helpless? or

Do we do it by being congruent? where people know where we are, that we can be trusted and that our meaning is clear?

Now looking at these forms through power "eyes" . . .

Power in Placating

You know what that power is . . . anybody who has faced the power of "I only want to please you, Dear," has probably experienced guilt, pity and contempt.

People feeling guilt, pity and contempt can't make loving contact.

People who feel guilt or pity toward someone are not likely to want to get close.

Real pleasing is a part of loving another person. It is important to distinguish between really pleasing and just trying to get on their good side.

Power in Blaming

Perhaps you have experienced facing this power, feeling fearful, often helpless and resentful . . . even murderous.

"Why in the hell are you always goofing?"

Fearful, helpless and resentful partners cannot make loving contact. People who feel afraid are not going to go toward the person they feel afraid of.

We need to be able to criticize, but it doesn't have to be done in a blaming way.

Criticism isn't necessarily pleasant, but it is *human* and it is essential.

Power in being Super Reasonable

Anyone facing this power can feel inferior and stupid.

"What is important is that one maintains their equilibrium. Losing equilibrium is costly. According to the latest research . . ."

Pummelled and overwhelmed by many long words, endless detailed explanations, and continual reference to the outside sources, it is easy to feel inferior, stupid and bored. People who feel this way are likely to avoid getting close.

Again, our intellectual abilities are essential to us. People need to be able to distinguish between using words as real information and making their "smarts" substitute for their value as people.

Power in Irrelevance

"Errors, errors, what interesting words. All birds have wet feathers." What did you say?

This kind of communication doesn't seem to fit anything. Its power is in its ability to distract and disrupt.

It often makes the other person feel off-balance and on-guard. At the beginning it might seem funny, but that soon wears off, and fear, anger, and rejection take its place.

We need the ability to be light and humorous, and we need to be able to change our directions. In irrelevance, the humor isn't funny and the meaning is clearly not understood.

I believe . . .

that people who use these forms of communication learn them while growing up, and that these are the best ways of survival they know, so they deserve my respect. I hope you also respect yourself for whatever you discover about your communication.

In my experience, I find people often do not listen to what they themselves say so they are not even aware that they are using these forms of communication. I find that most people do not want to come off in these ways once they recognize them. What people intend on the inside doesn't always show on the outside. Discovering this fact about ourselves is often a great shock. An experience with an audio or video recorder is a great way to find this out. However, maybe we have to go through a few shocks like this to get on solid ground with ourselves.

The results of interactions based on these forms of communication for both persons, is that each person, for different reasons, feels unloved, unwanted, alone, rejected.

These are expensive outcomes for human beings anywhere. How we maintain our survival is reflected in our communication and it becomes the setting for making contact. Ineffective as they may turn out to be, all these positions are efforts at creating self-esteem.

Like some medicines, though, they heal the illness but kill the patient. That is, they keep you alive, but not living. In all these forms of communications we are giving our power away to someone else in return for their giving us the means to survive.

No real human contact can occur in this way. This essentially results in developing relationships between people in which *both* are destructive, disappointing, and unloving. Self-esteem continues to be injured.

Relatively few people REALLY meet, so few things get creatively accomplished, and so few people feel secure about themselves or others. It could be so different.

There is communication which builds the self-esteem of the self and the other. I have given the name *congruent* to that form of communication.

Take a serious look at your own communication. How much of it falls into the descriptions of placating, blaming, being super-reasonable, or irrelevant?

Does this tell you anything about the kind of results you have been getting?

If you found that you do have these kinds of communication skills, don't fret . . . you are in good company! From where I stand, 95% of all the world uses them. That doesn't mean they're good, it only means they're familiar.

Power in Congruence

"Yes, I am feeling angry right now."

The power in congruence comes through the connectedness of your words matching your feelings, your body and facial expressions matching your words, and your actions fitting all. You come from a state of strength because all of your parts have flow with other parts. You are not blocking anything off.

You can easily be believed. Your energy goes to developing trust. You do not cause suspicion. You can be easily understood because you are clear. Other persons feel given to.

You feel open and can therefore feel excitement instead of fear.

You can live the *Five Freedoms*.

You know that you can choose, that you have many choices you can make.

This is the power that is in the seed, the power that creates ideas and ways to make things work better, the power to unite helpfully with others, power to make valid judgments, and the power to constructively meet destruction.

This power in turn makes it possible for you to have a healthy body, nurturing relationships, joy in things outside yourself and a happy soul, feeling you are living a meaningful life.

Getting things that are in the way out of the way

At first glance going in the positive direction really does sound easy and we could say . . . "Of course,—that's easy."

But if it is so easy, why aren't we practicing this more? The truth of the matter is that there are several things that get in the way that have to do with our insides . . .

Mrs. Jones, the Third Party, is one of them . . . Have you met her?

She is the third party in most people's lives. Over the years she has often been an unwelcome visitor in my life. She could be named Mrs. Schwartz or Mrs. Sanchez or Mrs. Anything . . . we all know her. Most of us have been taught to please Mrs. Jones at all costs on the theory that Mrs. Jones would be mad, or get hurt.

"I am the only one that goofs, worries, has bad feelings, has far out thoughts . . ."

and to mention them of course would kill me or you or, at the very least, would banish me forever from society . . .*and besides, Mrs. Jones wouldn't like it.*

What you don't think about is that Mrs. Jones also has a Mrs. Jones . . . and so it goes.

Discovering old rules

Most of us learned a whole set of rules when we were children that we are still using today unless we had some other experience to change those rules.

These rules are unrelenting bosses and compel strict obedience. The trouble is that these rules can't possibly fit all the situations we find ourselves in. We need guides, not rules.

The interesting thing is that most of us really try to live by impossible and inhuman rules and then feel guilty or angry because they exist.

Always eat all the food on your plate.

Never rock the boat.

Never speak unless you have something interesting to say.

Never argue with your elders.

Always take out the garbage at 6:30 p.m.

Always smile.

In the beginning these rules were usually learned to fit a special situation and then were generalized.

You can find out *your* rules by paying attention to all your *alwayses, nevers, shoulds,* and *oughts.* If you try to live up to them, I can guarantee you that you will have many experiences of failure and lots of guilty feelings about yourself and angry feelings toward others.

Just for an exercise, write down all your rules. Like most things, even hallucinations, there are some good grains among the chaff. Now let's transform your rules into useful human guides for you by adding a human context. For example, let's take a rather popular rule:

Never argue with your elders.

First statement:

I *must* never argue with my elders.

can change to . . .

I *can* never argue with my elders.

can change to . . .

I *can sometimes* argue with my elders.

can change to . . .

I *can sometimes* argue with my elders *when I have a difference of opinion.*

can change to . . .

I can argue with my elders when I have a difference of opinion and when I choose to.

Each of these additions represents a stage of risk and a new learning. It is something that really can be lived up to.

The last transformation gives you a human guide to aid you in the human situations in which you find yourself and frees you to make appropriate choices. You have saved the central subject but you have added the necessary parts so you can use it appropriately. It is helpful to have a *guide* about arguing.

If you were to try to live up to your rule, you could easily get ulcers and boils, and be thought of as rigid and unloving. All because you didn't want to disappoint your parents. After all, that's where you got them. Most of us don't want to do that, even though we make big noises on the outside that it would serve them right.

I have news for you: Your parents did not want it either.

One thing that probably happened was that your mother or father felt very insecure about their directions to you, or they disagreed with each other, so if you argued with them, it made them unsure inside. They felt like incompetent parents. They felt like that to begin with, but your arguing only made it show up more, or they didn't feel good about disagreeing with each other. So, if you shut up, lots of things could be avoided. You could not help but think it was a rule for life for you, when instead it was more a way that your parents had of managing when they felt bad at that time.

Living the catastrophic expectation

Most of us have great imaginations, mostly about the horrible things that may happen. We often get so busy with our imaginations that we miss the reality around us.

You didn't get to that appointment at six . . . You got there at six-thirty . . .

Your inside dialogue during that half-hour could have you getting ready for a divorce, getting fired, or entering a hospital.

"I am late..."

"What will he/she think?"

"He/she will hate me..."

"He/she will never be late..."

"He/she will probably fire me, leave me, bitch at me."

But then you would think:

"How can he/she do that when I've tried so hard?"

and then you would remember all the ways
you have been mistreated by that person . . .
or even the rest of the world.

"He/she has the nerve to be mad at me."

Meanwhile, you have gone through two stop
lights, almost run down a pedestrian, suddenly
realized that your wallet was home on the
table . . . The closest parking lot looks full, of
course. You are too upset to notice that the
sign says parking available . . . And when you
finally get there, the other person hasn't shown
up yet . . . and won't for another hour. The
whole thing has become a dud and look what
it has done to your insides.

Making appointments on time isn't a test of
love, it is a matter of convenience. Sometimes
we can't manage, so we bring some incon
venience. Nobody dies from that. It is only a
little unpleasant. Did you ever count the cost
to your body, your psyche and your life for
such foolishness?

You can see how this could work to make
contact difficult.

My past

Then there is my past . . .

Isn't it true that my past is a good indicator of me and a great weather vane for how things have to be for me? Forevermore?

After all . . .

"I was always weak"

"I never could succeed"

It is true that our past forms the foundation from which we operate in the present. Past experience is a powerful force. However, it is not true that we cannot change our present or our future. Many of us seem to believe that if we have pounded our head against the wall for the last thirty years, that is it, for the rest of our lives—our fate, so to speak.

Naturally, we do what we have learned, and if we haven't learned anything different than pounding our heads, then we will keep on doing that. Repeat performances of anything only mean that we haven't learned anything new. In some instances, what we have learned works well. No need to change. In others it works badly, so change is necessary.

The fact is we can learn something new any time we believe we can. Our bodies and our brains are equipped to do just this if we use them this way.

Change the way we look at things, and the way we act, and the outcomes will be different. Try it some time . . .

Another old saying of mine . . .

Is my past illuminating my present or contaminating it?

For example: Am I here at this time, now 40 years old, experiencing something going on as though I were only five, and am I back there instead of HERE?

Becoming acquainted with trigger words

All of us have some trigger words. These are words that make us see "red" when we hear them because they bring up a whole set of pictures and feelings from the past that were associated with pain, humiliation or shame, and then we automatically react as though that situation were repeating itself.

We fail to realize that the same word can mean quite different things to different people. Often needless physical and self-esteem injury occurs as a result.

The opportunity for contact can often be delayed or destroyed through this. No one can become so aware that they know the trigger words of every person.

In making good contact, loving persons learn about these words and avoid them, clarify them or eventually discard them. When goodwill abounds, the situation eventually rights itself. When ruptures are present, trigger words escalate the situation.

Find out what these words are for yourself and for those you love and see what happens.

Making assumptions

Assumptions are probably difficult to avoid. A friend showed me a negative potential of the word "assume." He said it makes ASS-U-ME. Pardon the vulgarity. I think many people are unaware of their assumptions.

We can't be absolutely clear all the time, but when doubts and distrust are present, checking the assumptions is a way to begin changing the atmosphere.

Many people do not seem to realize that very much of our thinking proceeds from assumptions often experienced as fact.

If we keep this in mind, it is easier to share your own and ask about the others.

"I am assuming . . ."

"Is that correct . . ."

"On what are you basing your conclusions?"

are ways of asking someone else for their assumptions or checking our own.

Often when assumptions are shared, misunderstanding and consequent hard feelings can be cleared up. Many of us seem to assume that because "I say" —*you hear—and you understand*. Many a potential relationship has floundered on that one. It may be initially tedious, but checking out what the other person hears is very important, especially when you have a doubt. The same word to two people can mean two quite different things.

Often it is very hard for people to understand others because their voices are too soft or their words are not clear. People sometimes seem to feel they will be thought ignorant if they don't understand. In that case, the only course open is for them to make something up. What is made up will be that person's fact, and things will proceed from there. I would rather be thought ignorant than foolish, so I take that risk now.

When this happens to me, I ask people to repeat, and I usually tell them I have not heard them clearly and I want to. Some people cannot hear well and so misunderstand. Much misunderstanding between people occurs because of these simple human behaviors.

"What I don't hear, I make up, and
I hold you responsible for it."

Differentness from another human being cannot be avoided because all human beings are biologically unique. This simply means that there are no duplicate persons.

Think about the fact that your fingerprint can identify you and you alone out of all the millions of people in the world. Individual whorls can be categorized, but the way they are put together on your finger is only yours. If that is true for your fingers, then it is true for the rest of you.

It is also true that any surgeon who learned his surgery can operate on any human anywhere because our physical parts are likely to be in the same relative place.

That means that with every human being we meet, we are guaranteed to meet sameness to ourselves and differentness from ourselves as a matter of human fact.

Recognizing this as a human fact instead of an outcome of hating or loving ("She is like me. I love her. She is different from me. I hate or fear her.") gives an opportunity to be an explorer with every person we meet which includes family members and friends especially.

From this point of view, the discovery of sameness can provide us with the security of familiarity, and differentness can provide us with excitement and new opportunities to learn and cope creatively. Limiting ourselves to valuing sameness only greatly reduces our possibilities for growth and increases the potential for boredom and destruction.

I made up an old saying to fit this:

We meet naturally on the basis of our sameness and grow on the basis of our differentness.

The key to the presence of sameness and differentness is appreciation, and the means to make it a real-life symphony is congruent communication.

Checking my awareness

It is very easy to get misunderstood. Here you sit, feeling all juicy inside, and someone acts as though you aren't there. More often than not, what is going on is that while you are aware of feeling your "juice" inside, your face appears calm and collected. You have not learned how to become *aware* of what your outsides are doing, therefore you feel misunderstood. Rejection often follows that.

Do you know how your face looks right now? Do you know how your voice sounds at this moment? You probably don't, but everyone looking at you and hearing you does. They take their cues, their mind reading, from your outsides. You are judging by your insides.

If you have a tape recorder handy sometime, tape yourself in a conversation with someone and then listen to it. If you happen to have a video or home movie camera, use it and then look and listen to it. Then you will see what other people see or hear. You will stand a chance of seeing how differently you come off compared to how you feel. It is sometimes a very jolting experience. This jolt is a cheap price to pay for more satisfying outcomes for yourself.

You, like many others, are probably very capable of feeling angry on the inside and putting on a happy face on the outside. You can't pull it off if someone really looks at you, except in very unusual circumstances where you have had long years of practice and a highly discriminate understanding of your awareness. So, when the other person says, "What's the matter?" as if something were wrong, you feel crushed, betrayed or misunderstood. You had expected a warm smile which would have matched your insides. What you got came from your outsides. If you don't have a tape recorder, a big help when this happens is to ask the other person what they saw or heard that made them say what they said. You will then get information, and you can say what you are really feeling. This will go a long way toward keeping things in balance. When misunderstanding occurs with me now, the first thing I ask the other person is to tell me how I looked and sounded to them, so I have a chance to add what is missing.

You own all the tools you need

Fortunately all of us have all the tools we need for making good human contact although we may not yet have *found* all of them.

In a nutshell, these universal human tools are your breath, your body, your facial expressions, your senses, your voice, your gestures, your words, your feelings, your past experience, your ability to move, time and space and other people. A whole contact involves using all of them so they fit together in a harmonious way (**congruence**).

We need to understand the condition that each of these tools is in, the uses we make of them—an awareness of when we use which for what; how to keep the tools in good condition, and how to extend their uses.

This depends on *knowledge* of how the tools work, *awareness* of how and when we use them, *patience* while we are learning and *practice* for greater skill. This suggests that there is more knowledge than what we already have, and more awareness than we are using. Learning to make contact has some similarities to learning a new sport. We usually get interested in a new sport because we feel it will benefit us in some way—make us healthier, happier or help us to get friends. Often someone else has turned us on to the possibility. We begin with a picture of excitement. Then, we start educating ourselves through reading about what we want to learn, getting a teacher, or associating with people who already have the skill we are seeking to learn. We often use a combination of all this depending on how we best learn. We look for opportunities to watch demonstrations, to listen to descriptions of what is involved. However we try to educate ourselves, we know we need PRACTICE to develop the skill we want to develop.

Learning to make contact has similar requirements. What I hope to accomplish in this book is for you to have a feeling that you really can learn how to make contact and a picture of how to make it possible.

Like all other skill learning, beginnings feel awkward, and often unreal. This is a necessary beginning phase because all new things we ask ourselves to do feel foreign to our body at the beginning. Do you remember when you first learned to drive a car? Do you remember how much you had to be PATIENT with yourself when what you wanted to do didn't quite match with what you were trying to do?

Your image of what you wanted didn't look like your picture of what you were actually doing.

Very few people in their childhood have had an emphasis on learning how to use their human tools to make contact with others and themselves. On the contrary, most of us were given repeated teaching on how to obey and how to do competent work. While these are skills helpful in many situations, they by no means cover all our human needs. Neither one of these teachings requires much honest contact with one's self or with one another. Most people have much of the new to learn and much of the old to replace when it comes to using their human tools for making satisfying contact.

None of us come with a little bag of directions about how to make contact. We do the best we can with what we have learned, as our parents, who were in the same boat, did.

If you can regard where you are now as the best you could do, then you can give yourself a big pat on the back for coming this far, and another one for changing to go further.

Changing is simple to understand, it just isn't easy to accomplish. There are many pitfalls in this seemingly obvious and simple idea.

How often have I noticed people who . . .

looked without seeing

listened without hearing

spoke without meaning

moved without awareness

touched without feeling

Most of us have paid a high price for this. The price is in not feeling good about ourselves and others, not feeling loved, not getting things done, and not having hope.

Often we feel helpless to do anything about it.

I think there are things we *can* learn that can help us do something about it. There is reason for lots of HOPE.

Everyone's head is fundamentally pretty good. The nice thing about learning is that when our eyes see it, and our brains say it makes sense, then, with patience and practice, like gravity, it falls into our guts and gets into our feelings and becomes a new learning— unless we work hard to stop it, like thinking "I am not worth it."

Using the senses

Our senses, which are mainly our eyes, our ears, our noses, our skins, and our mouths, are the main ways we have of taking in information from sources outside ourselves.

Few people have had much instruction in how to fully use their senses.

Seeing

I've heard a 60-year-old woman, a mother of a man now forty, refer to him as her baby. Same thing could go for a 40-year-old mother and her 16-year-old son. "Mother, see me as I am instead of how I was." Chances are if she has a picture of her son as a baby, she will be looking at him in terms of that picture NOW. Can you see what difficulties that makes?

We people are funny that way. We go from the pictures we form in our minds, which are often made up of our past experiences rather than our present view of the person NOW, this minute.

In addition, our eyes can play tricks on us because in childhood we learned all kinds of taboos, like... you shouldn't look at sexual things... bad things... and sometimes good things (if they were done by the wrong person).

Isn't it true that if you are looking at someone you are undressing them, or somehow invading them. Under these circumstances, the
decision is not to look. If we don't look, we
make it up. I, for one, would rather be the
receiver of what you actually saw instead of
what you made up.

Touching

In similar ways, the same thing goes for
touching. Ashley Montagu talks about skin
hunger, which all of us get mainly because
there are so many taboos against touching.
Our bodies, our nervous system, our satisfac-
tions with other people, and our creativity
might be greatly enhanced if we simply touch
more. Hands particularly can carry life-giving
energy when these hands have learned how to
be sensitive. Hands aren't only for work,
punishment, and sex. They are very much a
very believable human means of making
contact.

Hearing

Hearing has to do with listening.
    Are you aware that so many times, when
you are in the presence of someone who is
talking, you could be so busy with what *you*

are going to say next, or you are checking out
the right and wrong of the speaker, or that you
are preoccupied with someone or something
else . . . and you hear only fragments. In very
special situations this fragment sets off some
old fears or hopes attached to past experiences
that the following could happen . . .

*Speaker: I want to go shopping. Is there
anything you want?*

*You: What do you want to do that
for?*

Speaker: I can never please you.

You heard *shopping*—that set off your memory
that two days ago you went shopping for
everything you need. You remember saying
that to the speaker just yesterday. Now you
are irritated that he or she didn't remember.
"Besides he or she never remembers anyway so
what's the use . . ."

If you had listened to the whole thing and sup-
plied the information that was asked for and
then offered the information you had—it might
have gone like this:

Speaker: I want to go shopping. Is there anything you want?

You: No. I went shopping two days ago and I have everything I need. What is it that you want to shop for?

Speaker: Oh, there is a sale on shoes at the shopping center and I want to buy a pair.

You: I'd like to go . . .

Breathing

Many people are unaware that they are breathing shallowly and unevenly. I would like to suggest that you give real attention to your breath.

Take a moment to close your eyes, and just be in touch with your breathing. Your breath sustains your life and supplies oxygen to your body. The very act of paying attention to it makes your whole body and mind more receptive.

Repeat this exercise as many times a day as you can remember to remind yourself. It takes only a moment at a time. You are worth it.

See what happens.

Paying attention to words

Words are important tools for contact. They are used more consciously than any other form of contact. I think it is important to learn how to use words well in the service of our communication.

Words cannot be separated from sights, sounds, movements, and touch of the person using them. They are one package.

However, for the moment, let's consider only words. Using words is literally the outcome of a whole lot of processes that go on in the body. All the senses, the nervous system, brain, vocal chords, throat, lungs, and all parts of the mouth are involved. This means that, physiologically, talking is a very complicated process.

Our stimulus to use words comes from two places—from our insides and from response to something from the outside.

Here is a very simple model of how this works:

Something happens . . .

This primarily happens through the senses.

We hear something

see something

touch something

smell something

feel something

or move

either from the inside or outside

Then our brain gets busy to try to make sense.

The sense creates a feeling.

The feeling activates the Joy/Panic *button.*

Then rules or guides are called up to give direction about what action to take.

Learning how all this works and knowing how it works specifically with you can make a very great difference in your life and can help you come closer to taking charge of yourself.

More about words

If you think of your brain as a computer, storing all your experiences on tapes, then the words you pick will have to come from those tapes. Those tapes represent all our past experiences, accumulated knowledge, rules and guides. There is nothing else there until new tapes are added. I hope that what you are reading will help you to add new tapes out of getting new experiences

The words we use have an effect on our health. They definitely influence emotional relationships between people and how people can work together.

Words have power

Listen to what you say and see if you are really saying what you mean. Nine people out of ten can't remember what they said 60 seconds ago, others remember.

There are ten English words that it is well to pay close attention to, to use with caution and with loving care.

I, You, They, It, But, Yes, No, Always, Never, Should.

If you were able to use these special words carefully it would already solve many contact problems created by misunderstanding.

I

Many people avoid the use of the word *I*
because they feel they are trying to bring attention to themselves. They think they are being
selfish. Shades of childhood, when you
shouldn't show off, and who wants to be
selfish? The most important thing is that using
"I" clearly means that you are taking responsibility for what you say. Many people mix
this up by starting off with saying "you." I
have heard people say "You can't do that."
This is often heard as a "put-down," whereas "I
think you can't do that" makes a more equal
relationship between the two. It gives the same
information without the put-down.

"I" is the pronoun that clearly states "me"
when I am talking so it is important to say it.
If you want to be clear when you are talking,
no matter what you say, it is important to
state clearly your ownership of *your* statement.

"I am saying that the moon is made of red
cheese."
(This is clearly your picture)

instead of saying . . .

"The moon is made of red cheese."
(This is a new law)

Being aware of your clear use of "I" is particularly crucial when people are already in crisis. It is more clear to say "It is my picture that . . ." (which is an ownership statement). Whoever has the presence of mind to do this can begin to alter an escalating situation. When "I" is not clear, it is easy for the hearer to get a "you" message, which very often is interpreted as a "put-down."

You

The use of the word *you* is also tricky. It can be felt as an accusation when only reporting or sharing is intended.

"You are making things worse" can sound quite different if the words "I think" are added. "I think you are making things worse . . ."

When used in clear commands or directions, it is not so easily misunderstood. For example, "I want you to . . ." or "You are the one I wanted to speak to."

They

The use of *they* is often an indirect way of talking about "you." It is also often a loose way of spreading gossip.

"They say . . ."

"They" can also be some kind of smorgasbord that refers to our negative fantasies. This is especially true in a situation where people are assessing blame. If we know who "they" are we can say so.

How many times do we hear "They won't let me." "They will be upset." "They don't like what I am doing." "They say . . ."

If someone else uses it, we can ask "Who is your *they*?"

The important part of this is to have clear who "they" are so that inaccurate information is not passed on and it is clear exactly who is being referred to. Being clear in this way seems to add to everyone's security. Information becomes concrete which one can get hold of, instead of being nebulous and perhaps posing some kind of threat.

It

It is a word that can easily be misunderstood because it often isn't clear what "it" refers to. "It" is a word that has to be used with care.

The more clear your "it" is, the less the hearer fills it in with his own meaning. Sometimes "it" is related to a hidden "I" message. One way to better understand your "it" is to substitute "I" and see what happens. "It isn't clear" changed to "I am not clear" could make things more accurate and therefore easier to respond to.

"It often happens to people" is a statement that when said straight could be a comfort message that says, "The thing you are talking about has happened to me. I know how feeling humiliated feels."

To be more sure that we are understood, it might be wiser to fill in the details.

But

Next is the word *but*.

"But" is often a way of saying "yes" and "no" in the same sentence.

"I love you *but* I wish you would change your underwear more often."

This kind of use can easily end up with the other person feeling very uncomfortable, uneasy, and frequently confused.

Try substituting the word "and" for "but" which will clarify the situation. Your body will even feel different.

By using "but" the speaker is often linking two different thoughts together which is what causes the difficulty.

Thus "I love you, but I wish you would change your underwear more often" could be two expressions.

"I love you" and "I wish you would change your underwear more often."

It could also represent someone's best, although fearful attempt to make an uncomfortable demand by couching the demand in a love context, hoping the other person would not feel hurt.

If this is the case, what would happen if the person were to say "I want to ask something of you that I feel very uncomfortable about. I would like you to change your underwear more often."

Yes, No

A clear "yes" and "no" are important. Too many people say "yes, but" or "yes, maybe" or "no" just to be on the safe side, especially if they are in a position of power.

When "yes" or "no" are said clearly, and they mean NOW and not forever, and it is further clear "yes" and "no" relate to an issue rather than a person's value, then "yes" and "no" are very helpful words in making contact.

People can get away with much misuse of words when trust and good feeling have been established and when the freedom to comment is around. However, so often people feel so unsure about themselves that the lack of clarity leaves a lot of room for misunderstanding and consequent bad feelings. It is easy to build up these bad feelings once they are started.

"No" is a word that we all need and need to be able to use when it fits. So often when people feel "no," they say "maybe" or "yes" to avoid meeting the issue. This is justified on the basis of sparing the other's feelings. It is a form of lying and usually invites distrust, which, of course, is death to making contact.

When the "no" isn't clear, the "yes" can also be mistrusted. Have you ever heard "He said yes, but he doesn't really mean it."

Always, Never

Always is the positive form of a global word. *Never* is the negative form. For example:

Always clean up your plate.

Never leave anything on your plate.

The literal meaning of these words is seldom accurate and the directions seldom applicable to life situations. There are few cases in life where something is always *or* never. Therefore to try to follow these demands in all situations will surely end up in failure like the rules I described earlier.

Often the use of these words are ways to make emotional emphasis, like . . .

"You *always* make me mad."

meaning really . . .

"I am NOW very mad at you."

If the situation were as the speaker states, the adrenals would wear out.

Sometimes the words *always* and *never* hide ignorance. For example, someone has spent just five minutes with a person and announces,

"He is always bright."

In most cases the literal use of these two words could not be followed in all times, places and situations. Furthermore, they are frequently untrue. For the most part they become emotionally laden words that harm rather than nurture or enlighten the situation.

I find that these words are often used without any meaning in any literal sense.

These words are related to the inhuman rules I talked about earlier, so they have the potential for the same unnecessary guilt and inadequacy feelings because they are almost impossible to apply.

Should

Ought and *should* are other trap words from which it is easy to imply that there is something wrong with you—you have failed somehow to measure up.

Often the use of these words implies stupidity on someone's part . . .

"You should have known better."

This is frequently heard as an accusation. Sometimes it merely represents some friendly advice. When people use the words "ought" and "should," often they are trying to indicate a dilemma in which they have more than one direction to go at a time—one may be pulling harder than the rest although the others are equally important . . .

"I like this, but I should get that."

When your words are these, your body often feels tight. There are no easy answers to the pulls which "ought" and "should" represent. Biologically we really can go in only one direction at a time.

When your body feels tight your brain often freezes right along with your tight body, and so our thinking becomes limited as well.

Hearing yourself use the words *ought* and *should* can be a tip-off to you that you are engaged in a struggle. Perhaps instead of trying to deal with these opposing parts as one, you can separate them and make two parts.

"I like this . . ." (one part)
"But I should get that"

translated into . . .

"I also need that . . ." (a second part).

Such a separation may be helpful in considering each piece separately and then considering them together.

When you do this your body has a chance to become a little looser, thus freeing some energy to negotiate a bit better.

When I am in this spot, I can help myself by asking whether I will literally die in either situation. If the answer is *no*, then I have a different perspective, and I can more easily play around with alternatives, since I am now out of a win-loss feeling in myself. I won't die. I may be only a little deprived or inconvenienced at most.

Start paying attention to the words you use.

Who is your *they*?

What is your *it*?

What does your *no* mean?

What does your *yes* mean?

Is your *I* clear?

Are you saying *never* and *always* when you mean sometimes and when you want to make emotional emphasis?

How are you using *ought* and *should*?

For many people talking is a matter of habit . . .

as a result, people often don't listen to what they say. Unless we listen to what we say we can say all kinds of things we don't really mean and give out messages we don't intend. It sometimes becomes embarrassing when we are faced with evidence of this if we have no awareness of what we have done.

When something becomes a habit we stop paying attention to it. Our talk is of such great importance that I want to urge you to start paying attention to it—to bring back into your consciousness things you are actually saying.

Making contact with ourselves is finding ways to let ourselves know what we are doing, what we are saying, how we are moving and what we are thinking and feeling.

All of us learned things about how to be when we were growing up because it came so easily when we were very little. It was powerful learning. Much of that learning has now passed into habit and so getting in touch with what we are really doing now, is making what is habitual, conscious. This gives us a chance to discard that which no longer fits.

Once something is recognized . . .

"yes, I see it,"

and owned . . .

"yes, I do it,"

one has a picture of a new possibility . . .

"I see how it could be better"

then change can begin.

This process doesn't have to be grim. Make yourself an explorer using this book as a kind of map into yourself and the ways you make contact and see what kind of treasure, buried and otherwise, you can find.

Your world could look quite different.

Most of us speak in shorthand . . .

which we ourselves completely understand, and we wonder why "You, Stupid, don't understand me." Our shorthand is often accompanied by body messages which say just the opposite. Think of someone saying "yes" with their mouth and "no" by shaking their head.

What we really want to get across is our full meaning which results in *I understand you and feel understood by you*.

At first glance this might seem harder—especially since it is a new learning—for many people. Like all new learnings they begin with trepidation, awkwardness, and worry about the outcome. Learning to do this with persons you care about builds a firm foundation of trust and freedom. Then you can literally always find out where you stand with somebody and trust it. You can more easily say where you stand and make it clear.

I have been surprised by the number of people I have encountered who think they are not worth listening to or who are afraid of being looked at. I know some who do not even listen to their own words. Try an experiment for yourself. Tape record a discussion and listen to it to learn this astounding fact.

To help you on your way—put your life in a human perspective where:

the embarrassment of yesterday is the humor of today,

where:

what you thought would kill you yesterday turns out to be a whole new possiblity of today,

where:

the mistake of yesterday turns out to be learning, perhaps with some pain, for today

where:

the puzzle of yesterday turns out to be a solution today.

This is only to remind you that given some time, some hope, some new eyes, new effort, and some new knowledge and skills, many things evolve.

The problem is thinking that this moment is forever.

You have much more influence on making things change than you realize once you have decided to be your own decision maker.

You have this influence because you can:

See, hear, touch, feel, think, say, do, move, and *learn*

Channels

I have spoken about the most desirable physical position to accomplish congruence—being at arm's length and eye level, sitting or standing.

This positon makes it possible for all the channels for human communication to connect easily. When I am talking about channels I mean . . .

eyes / seeing one another

ears / hearing one another

mouth / talking

skin / touching

nose / smelling

If you look at me, and I look at you, then we can see each other. Otherwise we have to make it up. We can think about these channels as tubes that are moving things back and forth between people, like the ears do it through the airwaves.

If all my channels are working, my sight, my sound, my touch, my smell, my brain and my gut are all connected. They are all open and I hear something full and round. The muddy picture comes when someone is talking here and looking over there, or when somebody is talking to somebody and thinking about something else. It's the equivalent of one radio receiver in one ear and one in the other with each tuned to a different station.

That leaves the opportunity for people to feel mis-heard, mis-seen, mis-understood, and mis-felt, all consequences that lead to mis-contact.

Many people use mis-communication as an occasion to blame either themselves or the other. What I suggest is that this be used as a clue that the channels are not connecting and go on a search to understand what is happening instead of blaming, which will surely stop any further discovery.

When making such a search, ask yourself the question, "What did I see and hear, and what thoughts and feelings did I then have?"

Share this with the other person and ask that person to do likewise.

Just because I appear to be looking and listening to you, this is no guarantee that I am. All kinds of other things could be going on. There are many barriers to listening.

"I am sitting here because I don't want to hurt your feelings, or I fear punishment if I don't."

"Something very interesting over there is attracting me and therefore distracting me from you."

"I already know what you are going to say so I turn off my attention."

"I fear you are going to criticize me and I am defending myself."

"I am very preoccupied with worry about myself and I don't hear you."

"I have unfinished business with you and I can't hear you now. I hear you still from yesterday."

"I am not seeing you, but who you remind me of, so I hear their voice instead."

I call these unspoken but internally known parts, barriers to contact.

I suggest that all the barriers be removed by openly sharing that which is held inside and then clearing can occur.

This isn't always easy but it is very helpful if you can stick with it.

When I ask myself to speak in a way that I do not feel, I cloud my ability to see and hear and thus make difficulties in my contact.

It is also true that when I have to move my head down or up to look or hear someone, I put a strain on my body and hence cloud my own ability to hear and see.

Human beings are made so that our bodies flow in a balanced position and relaxed state. Any distortion of our balance causes us both to take in and give out incongruent messages. When we know that this is the kind of thing that can happen, then instead of blaming ourselves we look to other factors.

If we consider that we learned the most important things about how to be ourselves and how to relate to others (our parents) when we were children, then it seems easier to understand how so many of us feel our survival depends on others and we so easily give our power to someone else.

Your chances of really being seen and heard increase when you take responsibility for having yourself at arm's length position with anyone *including children* with whom you are trying to make contact.

Not doing this increases your chances for feeling little, weak, stupid, or even crazy. If you don't have a stool or a stair step handy ask your partner to sit down facing you. This helps to create a context where more self-esteem and equality can be experienced and where issues can be dealt with more clearly.

Unscrupulous people consciously maneuver other people psychologically by taking a physical position over them, like standing while the other person is seated.

How close or how far you are from another also has a significance. When two people are much beyond arm's length with each other, the feeling of the presence of the other person lessens and it becomes easier to act inhumanly and to hide . . . not exactly what contributes to making contact.

Many people seem to pay little attention to their literal physical positions when they are making contact. I think it is because people have not really thought about it.

Actually, sometimes position alone is the difference between whether one does or does not make contact.

Have you noticed, by the way, how often young children like to stand on chairs and tables. I think this is so they can be on a level with their parents. Eyes to navel doesn't make that kind of meaning.

Think of someone who is two or three feet
taller than you. Maybe, as an adult, you don't
experience this very often, especially if you
are tall. However, as children you met it
every day of your life. Your parents were taller
and bigger for at least eight to fourteen years.

Large size often inspires shorter persons to
feel threatened. (He is so big . . . I am so little.) It often awakens feelings of dependency.
(He can do anything. He can take care of me.)

Differences in size among adults often sub-
liminally reminds our body of the time we
were really little and helpless and our body
responds as it learned to do then, often much
to our pain.

If for instance you are taller or shorter than
your mate or any of your children or parents,
stand on something that will equalize your
heights and see if you feel differently.

When I have put all members of a family on
stools where they could be at eye level and
within arm's length of each other, parents often
seemed no longer to be so overwhelming and
children seemed to be so much more like people.

Your physical position in relationship to
someone else is an important part of making it
possible to make contact. Eye level, arm's
length puts you in the position in which contact is now more possible.

Now comes the matter of honesty—the first time can be very scary. It really is a risk. Being prepared to take this risk is the opportunity to choose the words that clearly spell out your ownership and thus give your partner the opportunity to hear you.

Accepting your Five Freedoms can help you have the courage to take the risks. Using words that clearly show your ownership will minimize the consequences of the risks.

A little summary . . .

If there is a map for making contact it would contain the following parts:

INVITING, first of all, someone to make contact with you. "I have something to tell you, are you ready to hear it? Can you listen now? I would like to talk to you."

"Have you a moment now, I need to share something with you."
"I have a bone to pick with you. Are you ready or will you listen?"

ARRANGING yourself in such a physical position as to be at eye level, arm's length, which usually means being seated because there are so many height differences between people.

BEING PREPARED to take risks for bringing your insides outside.

MAKING YOUR STATEMENTS beginning with "I": "I am angry" instead of "You make me angry;" "I am worried" instead of "You worry me." In short, you are dealing honestly by owning your statements and the feelings that go with them.

ASKING QUESTIONS, not the kind you ask when your child has his hand in the cookie jar right under your nose and you say "Are you taking cookies?" Of course you will be lied to. You are not seeking information nor will you get it. Questions are the ways to get information you don't have.

THINKING of all difficulties as opportunities for creating something new instead of the beginning of the toll of funeral bells. Each person can learn and grow from each creative handling of a difficulty. This may include dropping a burden as well as creating a new possibility.

Living the five freedoms

We live moment by moment. Each moment contains the possibility for new experiences, for opportunities to enhance our self-esteem, use congruent communication, change our rules and take more risks.

Suppose you had a computer that worked twenty-four hours a day and was always available. It was capable of registering all events of your life, past and present, with all your responses to those events, including all ways you made decisions, all your hopes, fears, and dreams. It could give back, upon command, any intellectual, physical, emotional, social and spiritual information regarding yourself that you wanted. In addition, it was capable of asking for any help that you wanted. It could feel human feelings, have human thoughts and perform human actions.

Would you feel *overwhelmed* by such a possession? Might you also be *excited* by the possibilities that were now in your hands? Would you feel *fearful* about the power that this computer represented?

Well, I think you own just such an instrument. I know I own one and perhaps like you, sometimes I feel overwhelmed, awed, and fearful as well as terribly excited about it.

Sometimes I feel it is a burden but more

often it is a fantastic resource place for me. You and I, we are human miracles capable of infinite growth. I think it is important to remember that in whatever condition we find ourselves—it deserves our love, honor, and respect. That will give the necessary nurture to develop the courage to go further.

What I have presented in this book are the means that some other people and I have found helpful in journeying through the mazes, unraveling the puzzles of our lives, learning to look at what is there and understand this beautiful miracle we call ourselves, to see with new eyes, to sort, to discard, and to add to what we already know.

I hope this will make it more possible for you to do things in "front of your face" rather than "behind your back," to be able to choose rather than feel compelled.

I wish you Godspeed and above all be loving to yourself.

BOOKS AND POSTERS BY VIRGINIA SATIR

YOUR MANY FACES offers Virginia Satir's central theme developed in more than 40 years as therapist, author, lecturer and consultant. She demonstrates that your many faces reveal the real you and she helps you accept them as the key to opening the door to new opportunities. 128 pages, soft cover, $5.95.

SELF-ESTEEM by Virginia Satir is a simple and succinct declaration of self-worth for the individual in modern society looking for new hope, new possibilities, and new, positive feelings about themselves. 64 pages, soft cover, $4.95.

MEDITATIONS & INSPIRATIONS by Virginia Satir, edited by John Banmen and Jane Gerber. For over twenty-five years, Virginia Satir has been conducting workshops around the world. In most of her sessions she begins by giving a simple, stage-setting monologue to the audience. These brief intros have become almost legendary among her followers as simple statements of a life-giving, affirmative credo. 96 pages, soft cover, $5.95.

The **I AM ME** poster is Virginia Satir's declaration of self-esteem, stating in part, that "In all the world there is no one else exactly like me and everything that comes out of me is authentically mine because I alone chose it..." 23" X 35", full color, $3.50.

The **FIVE FREEDOMS** poster offers the freedom to "see and hear," "say," "feel," "ask," and "take risks" and Virginia Satir explains how to see and hear, say, feel, ask, and take risks for a better you. 35" X 23", full color, $3.50.

On the **PEOPLE ARE MIRACLES** poster, beautifully illustrated with the silhouette of a ballerina, Virginia Satir's words are printed... "People need to see themselves as basic miracles and worthy of love." 23" X 35", full color, $3.50.

The **MAKING CONTACT** poster delineates Virginia Satir's belief of what is the greatest gift one can conceive of getting from anyone and what is the greatest gift one can give to someone. 23" X 35", full color, $3.50.

Virginia Satir offers **GOALS**, a poster providing the answer to loving, appreciating, joining, inviting, having, criticizing, and helping one another and thereby enriching one another. 23" X 35", full color, $3.50.

Available at your local book or department store or directly from the publisher. To order by mail, send check or money order to:

Celestial Arts
P.O. Box 7327
Berkeley, CA 94707

Please include $1.50 for postage and handling. California residents add 6½% tax